I Always Eat My Dessert First

Seven Days of Encouragement, Affirmation, and Reflection

I Always Eat My Dessert First

Seven Days of Encouragement, Affirmation, and Reflection

Rhondra O. Willis, Ph.D.

The Nicole Group

Published by Nicole Group, Inc.
Woodbridge, Virginia

Cover Design by Perfect Printing

I Always Eat my Dessert First: Seven Days of Encouragement, Affirmation, and Reflection
Copyright © 2014 Rhondra O. Willis
Published by Nicole Group, Inc.
Woodbridge, Virginia 22191

ISBN-13:
978-0692210598 (Nicole Group, Inc.)

ISBN-10:
0692210598

Printed in the United States of America

This book represents a seven day immersion into self-inspiration. The spiritual references and reflective exercises exemplify the relationship between inner strength and moving toward your life's purpose with deliberate intent.

Wanda Corner, Ph.D.
CEO, Corner of Success, Inc.

Acknowledgements

Father, Thank You for all your amazing grace and love toward me. I am truly humbled by your favor in my life

To my parents, Mrs. Sherrill Willis and James M. Willis (SMsgt, RET), I am so grateful that I belong to you. I could have not asked for better parents

Debra, my precious little sister, stay the course. I am so very proud of you.

Marvin, my dear brother, the soap fights were epic and now I CAN eat my dessert first!

Nikki, we have been friends for over half of our lives - LYLAS

Nett, your turn!

Kyla, Kris, Kein, Kam, Ryan, Jacquin, and Bri, hold onto God's unchanging hand. You cannot go wrong and He will never leave you nor forsake you

Mrs. Loretta Hill and Dr. Robert F. Hill, I was your first daughter

Mr. and Mrs. Grady Green, thank you for loving arms and a soft place to land

Mama Walker, I love you more!

Shanita, my other sister, I see you opening doors for other people. We thank you, I know it is not an easy task but your shoulders are strong. Don't forget to vote for yourself

Dr. Amola-Hill, I will simply say *Thank You*

Sandi, you cultivated my love for research and nurtured me along the way

Demar, I knew you were special when I met you. I can't wait to see what you do next!

Wan, Keep Going

Mr. Curry, your strength and energy amaze me

Felicia, you were right. Thank you for inviting me to share your space

Dr. Marshall, I will simply say *Thank You*

Daniel Circle Chapel Family, thank you. You are a constant in my life

NCIS Family, thank you. The lessons were invaluable

FOREWARD

I always eat my dessert first!!! When I was a kid, my dad would make me eat all my food, even when it was cold! Sometimes, I would not even get dessert and my brother would mercilessly tease me while he ate his dessert and I stared at ice-cold food. So, when I *got grown,* I vowed to eat my dessert first, simply because I could!!!

This is a story of love, lost love, painful love, and self-love through the Love of God. Realize that God still loves you no matter how many scars you have or no matter how many mistakes you have made in the past - He still loves you! What can separate us from the love of Christ...? Nothing! (Romans 8:35)

HOW TO USE THIS BOOK

This book is a Seven Day Devotional. I encourage you to use it often, write in it, share it, and grow! Every day is an opportunity to set the tone for your day. Take time to articulate your intentions and everyone (and everything) you are grateful for in your life.

You may find that your life will shift as you actively practice gratitude. I maintain a Gratitude Journal as I realize that it starts with Gratitude... *Practice Gratitude.* Gratitude is the ability to recognize a gift (not just a material gift) and acknowledge it. A gift can be a smile, a kind word, a compliment, a thank you card, time, or anything that you feel a sense of God's grace in your life. The more you practice giving and the more you practice gratitude, you need to run to keep up with His blessings and favor in your life. **Gratitude never goes out of style.**

Commit today to working to pour into someone else's life. God has blessed us abundantly and when we bless others, we bless Him. It is truly more blessed to give than to receive. **Generosity is life-giving to the giver and the recipient.**

T A B L E   O F C O N T E N T S

D A Y   O N E

CHALLENGE

You Can't Always Avoid Being Overcome by Events (OBE)

My Intentions for the Day_____

_____

_____

My Extreme Self- Care Commitment____

_____

_____

Most of our struggles are internal. Let it go. We are our biggest and most deadly opponent. We will find that sometimes it is just better to pay the tuition than try to finance life's lessons.

Sometimes it gets worse before it gets better. Have you ever done something with pure intentions but it seems like they just spun out of control and spun YOU up in the whirlwind?

It's not over until He calls it. Keep going

In yoga, as you deepen your practice, you begin to master the poses and your body. Yogis often find that the more they are devoted to their practice, negative effects may begin to surface. This may be a deterrent but as you grow in yoga and the sister science of Ayurveda you learn that this is part of the evolution. Practicing yoga is like life. You are competing only with yourself and striving for YOUR personal best.

This is also evident in the natural and spiritual world. Even if you are committed to the process and it seems to work against you, do not give up. The *old folks* used to say *keep living*. All that meant was that you would and could get through this stage in your life. There is nothing new under the sun but stay with THE Son.

One day, you will realize that some people and some situations really do not matter...

Confession: Today is like none other and if God is for me, who can be against me? I am aligned with God and His purpose for our lives. Amen.

REFLECTION

_____

_____

_____

_____

_____

_____

D A Y   T W O

YOUR INTEGRITY WILL KEEP YOU

My Intentions for the Day_____

_____

_____

My Extreme Self- Care Commitment_____

_____

_____

As for you, if you walk before me faithfully with integrity of heart and uprightness, as David your father did, and do all I command and observe my decrees and laws, I will establish your royal throne over Israel forever, as I promised David your father when I said, 'You shall never fail to have a successor on the throne of Israel. (Kings 9:4-5)

Tell the truth to your own hurt.

Have you ever done something and realized that you made a mistake? You get that sinking feeling that gnaws at the pit of your stomach. You are at a cross-roads. Do you *fess up* or just let it slide? This is the point where the rubber meets the road and you find out what you are REALLY made of…

The question that is never asked never gets answered... live fearlessly...Trust yourself to ask the questions that reveal the truth and true intentions... and then accept it.

Honesty and Integrity may cost you but it is worth it... Your voice is powerful; use it carefully...

Continue to take the high road, although it's less traveled, it is paved...

Remain worthy of your calling.

Serve with integrity even when you are wounded.

REFLECTION

_____

_____

_____

_____

_____

_____

_____

_____

_____

D A Y   T H R E E

SEASONS

My Intentions for the Day_____

_____

_____

My Extreme Self- Care Commitment____

_____

_____

Affirmation

I realized that all distractions are designed (custom made by the enemy) to make me lose focus on God. The big picture is that none of this has anything to do with me. I refuse to be swayed, feel sorry for myself, have pity parties or engage in negative self-talk. The enemy wants me to lose focus so I will not be in place for what God has for me. It's personal and this is between me and God. No matter what it looks like, I am firmly rooted in the Word and God's Promise for me.

God is continually gracious to us – even in the midst of a storm. When it seems like we are drowning, it will not consume you. Stay calm. The storm will pass. He is still writing the story. He is still the author and finisher of your faith (Hebrews 12:2). The end of the chapter does not mean that it is the end of the story, keep reading. It all counts! All the tears, all the heartache, the pain, the hurt... do not count it as robbery (Philippians 2:6). He will make it all come together for our good (Romans 8:28).

Prayer: Thank God for each of your tears, for they water your dreams.

EMBRACE THE EBB AND FLOW OF CHANGE IN YOUR LIFE. WE HAVE CONFIDENCE IN GOD THAT IN TIME, ALL THINGS WILL WORK TOGETHER FOR OUR GOOD...

Relax. It's going to work out. Stop trying to control it, influence it or rearrange it.

God's got it.

The passage of time can be painful if you allow it to color your vision. God's time is not like our time ... one day is as thousand years (2 Peter 3:8)... He will redeem the time (Ephesians 5:16-18).

He will level the playing field...
Champions do not tap out!

God only puts His best players in the game. Are you a star player or a bench warmer? Star players are not just lucky or talented; they work hard to get out front and run the ball – their team mates (your fellow Christians) are counting on you to score on the opposing team (the enemy).   Yes, someone is depending on you to do your part and play your position.

There are natural seasons in life. People enter and exit your life, sometimes without reason or your understanding. If someone fades from the fabric of your life, let it go black. Seasons are natural... you cannot force summer in the winter. It is ordained. Keep moving.

This is a season of refreshing, reconnecting, and love. Preparation is KEY in this season. God is shifting us to new levels with increased responsibilities. The seeds that you planted are beginning to take root and bloom. *As a man soweth... Sowing like sewing in the natural binds things together. God is not a man that He should lie (Numbers 23:19) - the Law of Sowing and Reaping is true.*

Just like we enjoy quality seasonings on our food, God gives our lives seasons to make life more favorable and enjoyable. Dig in!

Confession: No, my life is not perfect but He is perfecting (Psalms 138:8) His Work in me.

REFLECTION

_____

_____

_____

_____

_____

_____

_____

_____

_____

_____

_____

_____

_____

_____

_____

D A Y F O U R

BY DESIGN, NOT DISASTER

My Intentions for the Day_____

_____

_____

My Extreme Self- Care Commitment_____

_____

_____

Hold the Line: The Art of Timing

You are exactly where you should be at this very moment by design or default...

Sometimes (no, often), we may want to rush ahead of God and not wait for His timing. Timing is everything. We cannot rush ahead of His timing and expect optimum results. When we are TRULY ready, it will appear.

Confession: When I came to the end of myself, He was there…

You may be like me and are used to *making things happen* and when NOTHING happens, you are greatly perplexed and understandably frustrated. The bane of your existence becomes to conquer or master this *thing* that will not submit to YOUR will... So what does one do in this situation? You are enough and you have enough... start there. Take a DEEP breath, then EXHALE. Next, pray (you have not because you ask not) Mark 11:24-25. What now?

You Need a New Playbook

A Playbook is an often sacred, coveted book of instructions and strategies that are often born of proven experiences. They are fiercely guarded because the stakeholders know that if it fell into the wrong hands, they would lose their competitive edge and winning ability.

Your mature Playbook is critical as it provides a way to defeat the enemy as he seeks to steal your very life. Do not allow the enemy to grieve you about issues that are not about you or tied to your destiny. You can recover quickly with structured instructions, proven responses and reactions. In the face of adversity, He is your A-Plan and should be your only plan. Sometimes experiencing adversity is the only thing that will prompt you to move out of your comfort zone.

Wait for it, it will happen when you least expect it. **He is faithful** (1 Thessalonians 5:24).

Confession: I have tried it every other way; now I am ready to try it His Way, completely with no modifications.

Prayer: God order my steps. Let me be careful to stick to YOUR plan and resist the temptation to attempt to execute my plan.

REFLECTION

_____

_____

_____

_____

_____

_____

_____

_____

_____

_____

_____

_____

_____

DAY FIVE

My Intentions for the Day_____

_____

_____

My Extreme Self- Care Commitment____

_____

_____

STOP TRYING TO *FIX* IT. STOP INVESTING IN IT. IT WILL NOT PROFIT YOU

Have you ever loved someone with everything in you but they turned and walked away from you? I have been there, left with the pain, disbelief, wondering why he did not love you. If you think you are doing too much in a relationship; you probably are... balance is important. It is not very complicated, stop *spending* your precious energy if it does not align with your purpose. You cannot afford it.

Confession: *If I tell you that I love you; you may use it against me and leave me – alone.*

When the residue of everyone and everything else is gone... God is still there... When you look around and realize you are suddenly alone - fear not (2 Chronicles 20:17) for Lord is with you.

He is never surprised by any of your circumstances.

Commit to practicing extreme faith. You are still there because you have not mastered the lesson. It will only fully profit you after you master it and only then will you move onto the next level in God. What does it mean to profit? It means to gain over and above your investment.

Your investment or currency are your trials and your hard places.

YOU HAVE EMBEDDED RESOURCES TO FACE CHALLENGES

Sometimes you have to take a deep breath and just move forward into your destiny. Although it may be terrifying, be brave.

Have you ever looked around and realized that you had a lot of *stuff*? I have! But yet - I keep buying MORE *stuff*! I was inspired by a former student to begin my campaign of LESS IS MORE! We often hold onto things (or people) that we think we need to function in life. I have experienced the joy of releasing it willingly or I have held onto it for dear life, all the while it is squeezing the life out of me!

I began to look around and realized that I was buying the same *stuff* over and over again! If we just took a few moments to look around. we would realize that we already have everything we need! God is like that! He ALREADY gave you EVERYTHING you need to survive and thrive in this world. You are NOT ill-equipped to face life's challenges... We are often frustrated by life's challenges. If you define the word *frustrated*; it means *defeated* but you are by no means *defeated*. It is never over until God says it is over and if you still breathing right now; I would dare say that it is not over. I wanted NEW but I hung on to the OLD for dear life. Let it go. It has outlived its purpose and promise in your life. What may seem like a bitter end is often the beginning of sweet victory.

In that MOMENT that God has closed that door behind you! Amen and Amen!

D A Y S I X

MOMENTUM

My Intentions for the Day_____

_____

_____

My Extreme Self- Care Commitment____

_____

_____

It is the moment in which all the little things add up to your destiny and purpose.

*Do not allow the little foxes to destroy your living vines (*Song of Solomon 2:15)

When you refuse to allow the enemy *air time* - he signs off…

I finally got it. Stop it. Stop letting people slowly try to destroy you. After watching a beautiful interview of Dr. Maya Angelou by Oprah Winfrey, I got IT. Yes, people DID mean exactly what they said by their *off-handed comment* BUT I also had to check

17

MYSELF! Silver-gilded words are often razor sharp. Stop it! Those were the words that Dr. Angelou used when someone filled her space with negativity. I encourage you to think about your *own* words and intentions...

If you really think about the breakdown of a relationship (personal or professional), you can look back and find the root of its *demise*. How long you stay depends on when you *decide* to master the lesson. The key is not to UNDERSTAND your situation but your RESPONSE to it. Learn the lesson and pass the test! Rest in God! It's over when you say it's over...make up your mind.

Sometimes you just need to *shut it down.* Stop allowing people to waste or manipulate your time – no matter how much time you have invested into the relationship.

Do not abide (live) in toxic environments. Toxic environments have the potential to erode our very core. Develop strategies to protect your purpose and mission while on assignment.

Walk away – no, RUN as fast as you can...

Stillness (forced or voluntary) brings clarity. Sometimes we need to stop talking and just listen. We

discover what was always there. When you are quiet,
God often speaks...Listen

REFLECTION

_____

_____

_____

_____

_____

_____

_____

_____

_____

_____

_____

_____

_____

_____

_____

_____

_____

_____

_____

D A Y   S E V E N

CHANGE

My Intentions for the Day_____

_____

_____

My Extreme Self- Care Commitment____

_____

_____

CHANGE OR CRISIS REMOVES THE OPAQUE LENS OF FRIENDSHIP

Seven is a number of
completion or perfection

Your friends, acquaintances, and circumstances are
being re-arranged to meet the plan God has for your
life... do not fight it... flow in it. Limit the access of
those who do not align with your purpose. Go and
remain where you are valued. Become hard of
hearing when people try to spout THEIR negativity
into your life. Stop travailing and
just walk into your purpose.

If you listen long enough, someone will tell you who they are, whether you listen or not... Allow the tide of time to take dead relationships into your sea of forgetfulness. They cannot repay you for your tears, dark nights, and heartbreak - only God can repay you. Forgive them and move on... Learning to forgive is like learning to scuba dive, at first your breathing is focused than it comes more naturally without much effort.

It is natural to try to hold on to people as they pass through our lives - don't... Sometimes those things that appear as losses are really gains. Have you ever considered that God is stripping people from your life because the next thing you are going to do next REQUIRES your UNDIVIDED attention? Some people are uncomfortable with you when you do not fit into THEIR neat box. It's easier to deal with you in their limited perception than as you are...

MOMENT OF TRUTH: When you are honest with everyone but yourself, you still may attract those whom have a causal relationship with the truth.

What is critical to your success will eventually push its way to the surface. Consistency and Laser FOCUS are also critical to your success. Practice laser-like focus as it improves productivity and outcomes. What we reflect is least obvious to us.

Purpose is Powerful - use it wisely

If God gives you power, be careful not to misuse
it. *To whom much is given, much IS required.*

People do not change, they become as they really
are... do not let that deter your from your purpose and
your promise.   Your path becomes crystal clear
when you accept your calling and purpose. All the
inner struggles cease and you begin to breathe again.
Do not try to explain your purpose, it is a Divine
Assignment, handcrafted by The Great I Am for you.
Remember Dream Killers were once Dreamers too...
Allow their bitterness to make you better.

DO MORE OF WHAT YOU LOVE. YOUR GIFT WILL MAKE ROOM FOR YOU!

Vision

"Write down the revelation
and make it plain on tablets
so that a herald may run with it.
For the revelation awaits an appointed time;

it speaks of the end
and will not prove false.
Though it linger, wait for it;
it will certainly come
and will not delay.

"See, the enemy is puffed up;
his desires are not upright—
but the righteous person will
live by his faithfulness"
Habakkuk 2:2-4

I believe that visions are upgraded dreams with agendas. Adjusted perception gives you renewed vision. Do not get so caught up in your situation that you miss the lesson. If you are trying to recreate the past; you are missing the point. It is amazing how different your perspective becomes if you dare to venture further than you ever have before... The higher you go, the more your view will change.

Remember that anyone who has ever done anything great was never content with the view from the front yard. Dare to go a little further; you might be surprised to discover what lies just beyond your boundary. Stirring up the Gift requires disturbing AND reinvigorating what lies dormant.

Only when our dreams have focus and context do they have the ability to scare us.

TRUSTING GOD AND LEARNING TO FIGHT

Something inside of you shifts as you make a QUALITY decision to trust God in ALL aspects of your life. When you finally make a QUALITY decision AND commit to it; it will happen. It starts with TRUST. Trust Him. Detach your emotions from the situation and realize *it is just business*. HIS Business!!! Discipline and Focus teach you to make sound decisions that are not based on emotions. The principal thing is wisdom (Proverbs 4:7). Ensure she is gainfully employed.

When you change by realigning your mental and emotional boundaries; your situation will shift. I understand why and how people descend into that deep abyss. We are sometimes just one breath away, one breath that separates us from tragedy and despair. While dying inside, some people live for everybody else. It comes down to choices, deciding to keep breathing or just hold your breath. If you choose to keep breathing, then you must desperately purpose to get in and remain in God's presence. It is a hiding place where we are protected from life's storms. Even as you are tossed to and fro – hold on... even if your finger grips are screaming in pain – hold on...

Sometimes you will find yourself in an uncomfortable but familiar place and your first thought is not to fight but to take flight. The action of fighting is not necessarily violent but can be a stabilizing and peaceful action in itself. When your struggle is internal, you are in the fight of your life – for your life. Here is an important lesson that you must get: Don't run but stand your ground; it is your right, your God-Given Birthright. When you have charge over others, sometimes you let them learn the hard way. Well, now YOU are learning the hard way. However, it doesn't have to be hard but *endure hardness like a good solider* (2 Timothy 2:3) and *count it all joy* (James 1:2) because joy will eventually come in the morning (Psalm 30:5). ENDURE (outlast) the process. It is worth it!

God does not want you to be weak and unable to withstand every little wind that blows your way. STAND YOUR GROUND. It is good ground, watered and fertilized by your faith. Standing your ground requires maturity and will enable your growth in the Lord. *Yea, even though I walk through the shadow of death, I will fear no evil* (Psalm 24:3) it looks and feels like death but it is not the end of you. It is actually the beginning... as unto death. He does not want you to run from the enemy. He has empowered you.

Right now you might find yourself swelling up with courage and when you look toward what might lie ahead, you seize up with fear. Do not lose the seed that He planted in you; He intends for you to finish strong. He does not start anything He does not intend to finish (Philippians 1:6).

Do you feel that? The atmosphere is shifting! The door to your Destiny is swinging open!

Go ahead and walk into it!

To learn more about other books by
Rhondra O. Willis or learn more about her
work, visit our website
www.rhondrawillis.com

www.ingramcontent.com/pod-product-compliance
Lightning Source LLC
Chambersburg PA
CBHW070752050426
42449CB00010B/2442